NOTE
REALLY
SERIOUS

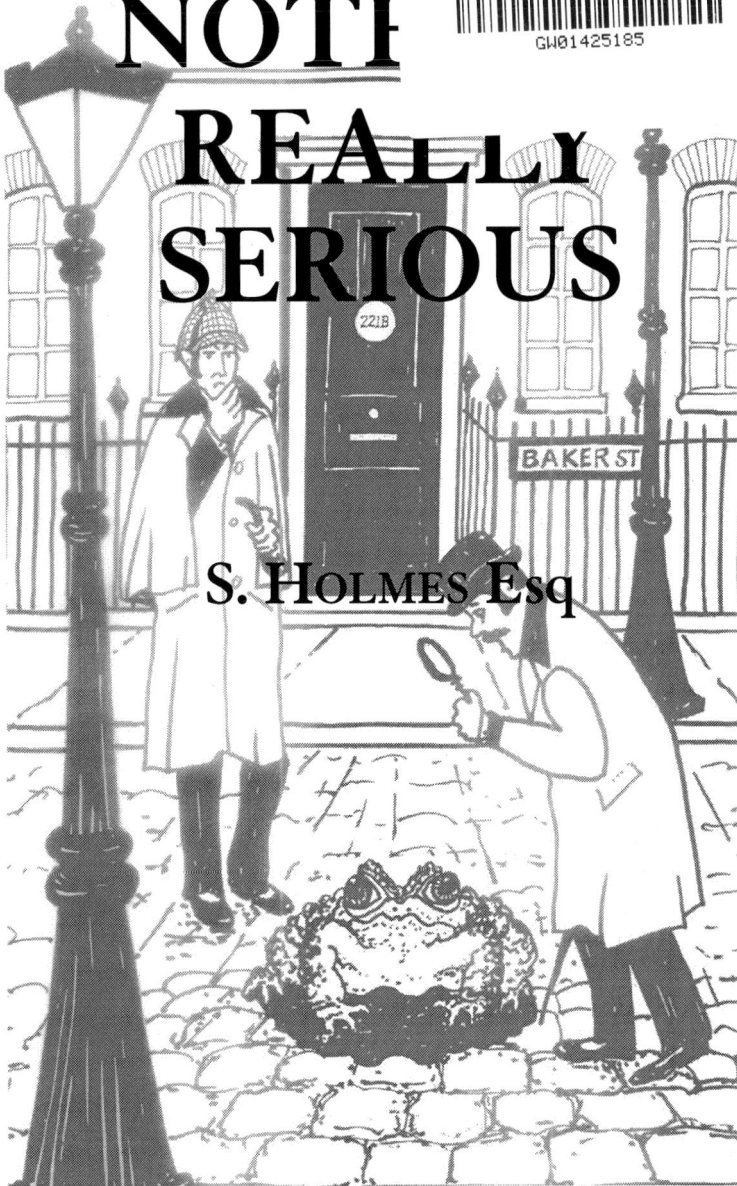

221B

BAKER ST

S. HOLMES Esq

TAGMAN

www.tagman-press.com

NOTHING REALLY SERIOUS

First published in Great Britain in the year 2002 by
The Tagman Press, an imprint of Tagman Worldwide Ltd,
in association with New European Publications Limited.

Lovemore House, PO Box 754, Norwich, Norfolk NR1 4GY, England
1888 Century Park East, Suite 1900, Los Angeles CA 90067-1702, USA
31 Denham Street, Bondi, NSW 2026, Australia
URL: http://www.tagman-press.com
E-mail:editorial@tagman-press.com

ISBN: 1-903571-15-4

A CIP catalogue record for this book is available from
The British library

Illustrations: Phyllis Dupuy
Printed by: LSL Printers Ltd, Bedford M41 0TY

TAGMAN

www.tagman-press.com

INTRODUCTION

Extracted from Dr Watson's Diary

It was shortly after breakfast that the letter landed on my doormat. It was from Mrs Hudson, our landlady at 221b Baker Street when Holmes and I lived there in the late 19th century, it read:

Dear Dr Watson,
I have found an old trunk in my attic which I believe belongs to you or Mr Holmes. As I am anxious to clear this area, I wonder if one of you could call to collect it, as it is taking up a lot of space at the moment. Please let me know when it will be convenient for you to call.

> *Yours sincerely,*
> *Mrs M Hudson.*

I was unaware that either of us had left anything behind when Holmes retired to Sussex to keep bees, and I returned to my practice in Kensington. However, I was intrigued to find out what the trunk could possibly contain, so I replied that I would be free to call on the following Friday morning, which was the earliest that I could get away from my surgery.

I was delighted to find Mrs Hudson still in the best of health, and without much ado, she showed me upstairs to the rather musty-smelling attic, in one corner of which was a large trunk which I do not recall ever having seen before.

'I'll leave you to it, Doctor,' said Mrs Hudson, as she closed the door and left.

Inside the trunk were some of my old army papers, a letter from the hospital discharging me after treating my Afghan War wound, several bills and receipts, and – hello, what's this? A carelessly bound manuscript entitled *Nothing Really Serious*, by S.Holmes.

I wasn't aware that Holmes had ever written anything other than the odd monogram about characteristics of different types of ash, so I began reading it....and reading it – and I couldn't put it down until I had finished.

The manuscript certainly did not belie its title – I had no idea that Holmes was such a humorist. Certainly, he could add a touch of irony and even sarcasm to many of his remarks, but I had never imagined him capable of writing in such a humorous vein.

This, I thought, deserved to be published. And I knew just the person who could do it.

I went downstairs and assured Mrs Hudson that I would make arrangements for the trunk to be collected the next day, and took a train to Norwich in Norfolk to see my friend Anthony Grey, a former Reuters correspondent who had become a publisher. He shared my enthusiasm about the book, and said that his impress, The Tagman Press, would be happy to publish it.

Trying to contact Holmes was rather more difficult – he being in the heart of deepest Sussex and rather loath to involve himself in anything which may bring him unwanted publicity. Finally, I tracked him down to a village not too far from Burgess Hill, and persuaded him that publication would be a good thing. I think that he felt rather flattered that his manuscript was receiving such attention.

I hope that you enjoy reading it as much as I did.

John H. Watson MD
Kensington, London

ACKNOWLEDGEMENTS

My grateful thanks go to Mr Mike Digby, Mr John Coleman and
Mr Anthony Grey, without whose assistance and support this book
could not have been published, to Phyllis Dupuy who created the
splendid illustrations and to Mrs Marcelle Shulman of The Sherlock
Holmes Memorabilia Company, whose enthusiasm for the project
has ensured the book's success. And of course, to the late Sir Arthur
Conan Doyle, without whose genius and imagination neither I nor
my good friend Dr Watson would have existed at all!

S. Holmes Esq.
Baker Street, London
August 2002

A STUDY IN SCARLET

Dr John H Watson and I first met
Through a mutual friend, Stamford, to whom I owe a debt
Of gratitude for bringing me a friend
Who was loyal and trustworthy to the end

He helped me capture the German varlet
Whom he featured in his story: A Study in Scarlet
Occasionally angry, and sometimes furious
When he found my manner decidedly curious

It took him a while – 'twas almost an obsession –
Before he discovered my true profession:
Though my general knowledge is somewhat defective
I am the world's only consulting detective.

HOUND OF THE BASKERVILLES

Many theories still abound
About the dreaded Baskerville hound

That evil creature who tried to kill
The hapless Sir Henry Baskerville

The Dartmoor beast with teeth like sabres
Kept by Sir Henry's manic neighbours

No doubt this tale kept all agog –
But it was just a dirty dog.

TOAD

There is a toad
At the end of the road
At the end of the road
A toad

But what is he doing
That toad
At the end of the road?
Has he come a-wooing?

Of course not
And if you keep pondering long enough
You'll find that your head
Is a-spinning

The only reason why the toad
Is at the end of the road
Is because he's not at
The beginning

NEAR MISSES

It's the latest craze and catching on fast: phrases or titles which never quite made it, such as:

Fiddler in the Porch

Pop Goes the Penguin

The Grapes of Pique

Charge of the Dim Brigade

Lady Chatterley's Boyfriend

6-up

Gone with the Breeze

Cloud Eight

The Van Allen Cummerbund

Sixth Heaven

Insubordination on the Bounty

The Man in the Wooden Mask

Dr What

Moby Phil

The Lady of Spring Onion

Who's Afraid of Louisa May Alcott?

An Early Summer Day's Dream

Love in a Lukewarm Climate

The Hair Stylist of Seville

Madam Caterpillar

A Businessman of Venice

From Russia with Friendship

Continue Trucking

H Claudius

The Quality of Mercy is Lumpy

Bubble, bubble, toil and irritation

La BoheL

Give Me Liberty or Kill Me

Robin Cowl

Give My Regards to the Avenue of the Americas

The First No-K

Monty Cobra's Sailing Big Top

An iron drapery has descended across Europe

John the Ripper

Ku Klux Klub

The Legend of the Plastic Mountain

The Boston Wine & Cheese Party

Man and SuperApe

The Seven Deadly Misdemeanours

3.14 in the Sky

The Ingoldsby Rumours

The Dressing Gown Game

I Almost Did It My Way

Hawaii 4-9

Rin-can-can

Singing in the Drizzle

The Mongrel of the Baskervilles

No Man is an Isthmus

Swan Pond

A stitch in time saves eight

Beyond the Azure Horizon

Fawlty Minarets

The Mad Cobbler's Tea Party

$3^1/_2$ - leaf clover

Puss in Shoes

$6^1/_2$ Pillars of Wisdom

Alice in Miracleland

Half a loaf is better than one slice

Snow White and the Seven Undersized Lumberjacks

FIRE

It was two o'morn in the clocking
When fire the break out did
And the high rose flames and shocking
'Ere you could eye a batlid

The take off was girling her stocking
The reading was student Euclid
And the vicar was bishop unfrocking
Bethings of the cause that he did

The firethen came men a'knocking
With flames for the water to rid
And the match with a man stood a'mocking
He'd light it a-set for ten quid

And away in the stood distance rocking
With a him behind body quite hid
Was the folks for the all reason flocking
Some fireworks wanted his kid.

WRONG TIMETABLE

What did the doctor say about the bus conductor's wife who had triplets?
    'Typical of London buses – you wait ages for one to arrive, then three
come along at once!'

NIGHT EXPRESS

ANNOUNCEMENT: Now it's time for the news from our NIGHT EXPRESS studio. Your newscaster: Stewart Quentin Holmes.

SQH: First the footlines –

CAESAR ASSASSINATES ROMAN SENATORS
AMERICA DISCOVERS COLUMBUS
MANY DIE IN BAGHDAD CARPET CRASH
SULTANA SCHEHEREZADE FLEES TO WEST AND
SEEKS POLITICAL ASYLUM

Good evening. Finally, to end the main items again, here is the news.

The Roman emperor Julius Caesar stabbed and killed all the members of the Senate single handed in Rome today. The massacre came 24 hours after Caesar had made a major policy speech in which he warned senators to beware the tides of March, but as it was April, it appears that this warning was ignored. Later he made a nationwide broadcast on Rome Radio in which he said: 'I come to raze the Senate, not to bury it.'

America has discovered Christopher Columbus. A spokesman for the State Department in Washington said today that Columbus was found cuddling his ship, hiding in a broom cupboard under the stairs at the White House. 'I always knew that there was another country here somewhere,' he declared.

In Tokyo, Madame Butterfly was granted a decree nisi in the Divorce Court today on the grounds of her husband's adultery. Mr Butterfly was alleged to have taken up residence with a Miss Kate R Pillar on the same leaf at Mulberry Bush.

In a cross-petition, Mr Butterfly alleged that his wife was in love with a certain Lieutenant Pinkerton, whom she had promised to marry on his return from manoeuvres overseas.

In his summing up the Judge said that although there was no doubt that Madame Butterfly had, in recent months, been rather flighty, her husband was obviously a fly-by-night.

This year's Ignoble Prize winners were announced from Stockholm today. They are:

Big Chief Sitting Bull for his services to brain surgery
Hannibul for his researches into zoology
Genghis Khan for his services to peace
Jesse James for his researches into bank security
Bluebeard for his services to monogamy
Blackbeard for his services to freedom on the High Seas, and
Captain Bligh for his efforts to alleviate human suffering.

Reports are coming in about a serious air crash at Baghdad. It is understood that 33 people were killed instantaneously when a carpet overshot the runway at Baghdad Carpetport and crashed into the sand, just missing a camel train on its way to Basra.

Among the dead were the crew of three – two pilots and a stewardess. There were no survivors.

The pilot's last message to Air Carpet Control reported that No.1 Fringe and Tassel were on fire, and he was preparing for an emergency landing.

One eyewitness, who was nowhere near the scene at the time, said that passengers stood no chance as the carpet came weaving down. Many fell off before it hit the ground.

The Air Carpet Controller has issued instructions for the immediate recovery of the carpet's black box before it disappears in an imminent sandstorm.

First indications suggest that the fire was caused by lighted hookah which overturned in the non-smoking compartment.

The Austrian composer Johann Strauss says that he is writing a sequel to *Die Fledermaus*. He intends to call it *Die Fledercat*.

He told our correspondent that his future plans would include operas entitled *Die Flederdog*, *Die Fledercow* and *Die Flederhorse and Cart*, but before doing this he would spend several months at George Orwell's animal farm to do vital research.

The well-known conductor Leopold Orchestravitch was shot and killed when a cannon was fired during a performance of Tchaikowsky's 1812 Overture at a Promenade Concert at the Royal Albert Hall last night.

The leader of the orchestra reported that Orchestravitch was still conducting two minutes after his death.

A concert official said later that all future performances of 1812 would contain no gunpowder and that all cannon balls would be blanks. It is expected that this ruling will apply also to 1813.

And at Bridler's Wells last night the opening performance of one of Tchaikowsky's ballets had to be cancelled when prima ballerina Eliza Dancelittle was drowned when she fell into the Swan Lake. Said impresario Monsieur Pasdedeux: 'We intend to tighten up safety regulations so that in future all ballerinas will have to wear flippers.'

The Sultana Scheherezade, beautiful wife of the Sultan Sharyar of Persia last night escaped from the Sultan's palace and is reported to have asked for political asylum in Italy.

Police from 40 countries belonging to Upterpol have been called in to search for the runaway queen.

Our reporter Percy Crackpot in Rome says that Scheherezade is reported to be staying at the home of the artist Leonardo da Vinci who, captivated by her smile, has asked her to pose anonymously for a portrait to be called the Mourner Loser, for a queen who mourns her lost throne.

Now sport: racing – a Trojan horse won the Greek Derby in Athens today by four furlongs, but it had to be disqualified when it was discovered that it was made of wood, and was being ridden by 500 Greek soldiers.

Fishing – Five-year-old Ronald Line of Yorkshire has caught a 60ft long whale in the Firth of Forth and Fifth in Scotland.

When interviewed by our fishing correspondent he said that he had used neither rod nor net. 'I read Moby Dick to it, and persuaded the fish to come ashore,' he said: 'I want to keep it as a pet, but it won't fit into the bath.'

Swimming – Ivor Squid won the Southern Counties Diving Championship at Portsmouth today, but the award will be presented to him posthumously since he failed to surface.

Finally the weather: we regret that owing to certain difficulties at our Meteorological Office, the weather has been cancelled.

That's all from us. Good night.

ALIENS

Have you ever thought
That while we, in our mirth
Wonder if there's life on other planets
Other beings on other planets
Are wondering if there's life on Earth?

Perhaps they can see clouds, water
Or vegetation
Or maybe Charing Cross, London Bridge
Or Waterloo station

What do they look like
These beings from Outer Space?
And how do we appear to them
We members of the Human Race?

Maybe they think we're monsters
With TV aerials in our heads
Or perhaps we look like insects
With beady eyes and a hundred legs like centipeds

Just fragile human beings
They probably could never conceive of
Before they leave whatever planet
They're planning to take leave of

So if ever the subject of
Life on other planets
Comes up in conversation, don't mock it
Because if alien creatures do land here
You're liable to get a rocket.

IMAGINE THAT

Professor Orlyn de Mynd, president of the Halluci Nation (the nation of Hallucis) took his imaginary seat at the Untied Nations Insecurity Council yesterday as his country was sworn in as a new member.

At an earlier press conference, his press attache, Dr I M A Mirage, said: 'The main object of the Hallucis is to promote world dreams, but as yet we are not quite all there.'

Then he walked through an imaginary door and disappeared.

The Hallucis' ambassador to the UN is the well-known diplomat I M Chester-Dream, whose woolly-headed thinking is well known in political circles. 'We shall probably get around to making a real contribution to the world some time,' he said dreamily.

NO END TO IT

One thing that you can never say about Schubert's Unfinished Symphony: that it was a COMPLETE waste of time.

PEOPLE AND THINGS

People and things
People and things
I'm always hampered
By people and things

People in crowds
In the stores and the streets
At bus stops and lamp posts
And wooden bench seats

All these things hamper
My progress each day
Why won't they ever
Get out of the way?

People and things
People and things
I'm always hampered
By people and things

Buses, cars, taxis and
Lorries and vans
Pedestrian crossings and
Holdups and jams

Traffic lights, police cars
With sirens and rings
One-way streets, cul-de-sacs
Railway sidings

Post boxes, call boxes
Meters and trees
Animals, children and
Shoppers on sprees

Life would be happy
If only, I say
People and things would
Get out of my way!

MEMORY

Memory is a wonderful thing –
For those possessing it
For everyone else
It's simply a matter of guessing it

Sometimes I can remember things
That happened long ago – or even longer yet
But mostly for important items and
Other matters absolutely vital I'm bound to forget

Some say that I have
A memory like a sieve
And probably I shall continue to have one
As long as I live

There are times when I'd rather forget certain days.
Like from January to December
But more often than not it is just these days
That I'm most likely to remember

Well might you say: Oh, that's
Just the way it is
But ninety-nine times out of ten I don't really know
What day it is

It's easy to remember the good times
The romances, the thrills
Because there are so few of them – and the
Rest of the time is taken up with paying bills

Sometimes I wish I could have
Instant recall – just like a computer
But if there is a method of acquiring this ability
I wish I could find a tutor

How does one attain the knack of remembering things
That you want to remember, and forgetting what you want to forget
When events are happening all the time –
And think of all those which haven't even happened yet

It might help to keep a diary
Or find a handkerchief and tie and knot in it...
There was going to be a last line to this poem
But I've forgotten it.

EPITAPHS

Here lies the body of Jonathan Quayle
Whose faith in the Lord led him to jayle
Because he believed, as he lived by stealth,
That the Lord helps him who helps himsealth.

Here lies the body of Smitherson Quong
Who died at an age so very yong
His full name was Smitherson Mathieson Quong
They called him Smithers for short
But not for long.

IN FOR THE KILL

I tried to stab her yesterday
With the kitchen carving knife
But she moved towards the oven door
And that move saved her life

I tried to shoot her yesterday
The bullet went too wide
I'd fired right on target, but
She'd stooped to a child that cried

I tried to hang her yesterday
It wasn't any use
Just as I drew in the rope
The wretched noose broke loose

I tried to axe her yesterday
It wasn't worth a candle
I'd brought the chopper down and then
The blade flew off the handle

I'm in a prison cell today
And rue Fate's cruellest joke:
Just now she fell under a bus
Which killed her – at a stroke.

NEWSFLASH

The Duke of Wellington has defeated Napoleon at Waterloo. 'I gave him
the Order of the Boot.', he declared.

THE FINAL PROBLEM

The mad Professor Moriarty
Is not the type to invite to a party

Known as the Napoleon of Crime
He'll try to trick you all the time

The same goes for his right-hand man
Colonel Sebastian Moran

But if his manner really appalls
Just throw him over the Reichenbach Falls

RADIO PREVIEW

Now we look ahead to the rest of this evening's entertainment:

In a few moments we shall have A Book at Bedtime. Tonight's book is The Concise Oxford English Dictionary, recited in a droning voice by the Archbishop of Canterbury.

After that there is this week's soap opera, in which famous bars of soap will be singing Handel's Water Music from the newly-opened opera house at Bath.

Cussens Imperial Leather takes the lead – although as yet there is no dog – and Pears soap gives a transparent performance opposite Camay and Wrights Coal Tar.

Finally, tonight's mystery thriller, Death in the Sea, in which detectives investigate the extraordinary deaths of various fish killed in a clinical manner suggesting that the killer may be a member of the Royal College of Sturgeons.

Police are looking for someone who calls himself Jack the Kipper, who has been giving the authorities quite a few haddocks lately.

All this is rounded off at midnight with the news and weather – that is, whether or not we shall be back again with you tomorrow night.

DAY OF DISASTER

More than 500 people have survived, some of them seriously, a jumbo jet crash said to have been one of the worst rail disasters in shipping history.

The plane, the SS Megalomania, ran aground when it crashed into a mountain peak some 40 fathoms beneath the Atlantic Ocean while crossing the Kalahari Desert en route to Hong Kong. Many were hurt, but several people were taken to hospital suffering from a severe lack of ill effects.

There was no emergency message from the train's captain or the ship's fireman before the vessel crashed, and a major rescue operation has been launched to complete the plane's destruction and wipe out any survivors.

One eye-witness (a witness with one eye) who was nowhere near the scene at the time, said that wreckage from the craft, which remained intact on impact, was strewn for several inches around. 'I saw a big explosion, but heard absolutely nothing,' he declared.

An inquiry will be held into the effect of the crash and the survival of so many passengers.

RETIRED

Do you know why Rip van Winkle didn't wake up for so long? Because it was ASLEEP Year – naturally.

GULP

If one swallow doesn't make a summer, how much do you have to drink before you get a heatwave?

ROVING SPIRIT

The graveyard is my favourite haunt
It's the dead centre of town
But you might gain a stone or two
If you dare to go too far down

Most people are dying to get there
They must think it's good for a laugh
But there aren't many people to greet you
There's only a skeleton staff

I've joined an underground movement
There's always a good plot or two
And accommodation's no problem –
I have a tomb with a view

And with every new day that's dawning
Your own turn will come all too soon
So forget about weeping and mourning –
At least until the afternoon.

PLUCK OF THE IRISH

That well-known Irish teetotaller, Drunkas O'Lord, reports the introduction of a new member of the IRA. As he entered the secret headquarters, other members introduced themselves: Sean O'Flannagan, Seamus O'Hara, Patrick O'Hagan, Paddy O'Reilly.

The new member thought for a moment, then said: I'm Heter O'Sexual.

LUNCH IN HARMONY

It was a beautiful day, with the birds shining and the sun twittering in the trees, as the express train thundered through the tiny village of Notts Topping. Nothing ever stopped at Notts Topping.

As couples kissed beneath the shade of the Uppagum Tree, and cattle grazed lazily in the hazy maize, a party of musicians from the Little Codswallop Somephoney Orchestra were on their way to their annual orchestral outing for lunch.

In a country restaurant at Boggedown-in-the-Marsh, the musicians waited for their famous conductor, Ivor Baton, to wave them to their seats. Lunch was served on music stands.

On the menu were flute juice, symphony soup, spaghetti polonaise, lamb Chopin chips or crotchet potatoes, fried treble clefs and chips with fanfare sauce, French horn on the hob, mustard and clefs or percussion peas, Pizzacatto pie with Beethoven salad and Rachmaninoff potatoes, string quartet steak in violinseed oil.

This was followed by trombone trifle, concerto crumble, Strausswaltzes and cream and Hungarian Rhaspberries. Later came cantata coffee, Brandenberg and cigars. As lunch was on a low key budget, some guests settled for cocktails such as Rossini dry, Ave Maria sherry, or just a gin and tonic solfa. As the conductor said later: 'If music be the food of love, have a sonata sandwich.'

PER ARDUA AD NAUSEAM

I have never really thought a lotto
Having a coat of arms and family motto
Since my knowledge of heraldry matters
Lies ruined in fragmented shreds and tatters

Noble efforts by noble earls
Produce wit and wisdom with such pearls
As described their various ranks and attitudes
With phrases such as 'For King and Country' –
    and other platitudes

The Prince of Wales, son of the Queen
Has chosen the German phrase 'Ich Dien'
It means 'I serve' – an odd choice or whim
Because soon the country will be serving him

Americans, too, can cut a dash
Displaying in stores with such panache
Notices warning customers rash
'In God We Trust – Everyone Else Pays Cash'

Aristocrats from here to Prestatyn
Often choose a phrase in Latin
To declare to all and sundry
Such as 'Sic transit gloria mundi'

Of what point are these pithy phrases?
They're not just one of those modern crazes
Which peter out before too soon
Like the phases of the moon

Are they meant for inspiration
Of a serfdom or a nation
Are they war cries or words so bold
For family traditions to uphold?

Many a woman's displayed her charms
To a man with a natty coat of arms
And left him lying, completely blotto
Muttering deliriously the family motto

How well I remember old Ponsonby-Smythe
I doubt if the fellow is still alive
But he was determined his motto would awesome be:
'Honi Soit Qui Mal y Ponsonby'

THOUGHT

There's a school of thought
Which thinks that all thoughts
Have been thought of before
By some kind

Of all-thinking, thought-storing
Thought finding thinkpiece
Known as the
Universal Mind

And if you've thought before
That the thoughts which you thought of
Were thoughts which only you
Could find

Then think again –
Because all the thoughts which you've thought of
And even those you've left behind
Are part of the Universal Mind

So having thought of that thought
Why think of another?
It's bound to become
Such a bore

Because every thought
That you ever think of
Has already been thought of
Before

TOXOPHILITE SCHOOLS

I shot an arrow
Into the air
It fell to Earth
On Eaton Square

Now there's a school record
That can't be beaten –
The day that 'Arrow
Fell on Eton

PROVERBS

Many a true jest is spoken in words
He who laughs last is too dim to see the joke

There's many a slip twixt skirt and hip
A bird in the Strand is worth two at Shepherds Bush

All the world loves another
People who live in stone houses shouldn't throw glass

'Tis a long lane that hath no parking space
Music hath charms – and so hath bracelets.

THE CENTRE OF THE LOONYVERSE

I suppose that it is only unnatural that on such an imperfect winter's day, with the birds shining and the sun twittering in the trees, one's thoughts should turn to Father Nature and the reason why things are as they aren't.

It wasn't so long ago in the future that people believed that the Earth was the centre of the Loonyverse (which in one sense may still be true). Although Leonardo Dawhiskey (who painted the Moaning Lizzie) came up with some evolutionary ideas, it wasn't until old Copperknickers declared that the Earth moved round the Sun that he was taken to task by the Spanish Imposition. Well, I mean, if you'll believe that you'll believe anything; although why only the Spaniards were so concerned about it is rather odd, as they were the fellows who were supposed to know their onions.

Still, I suppose that religion reared its ugly head once again where science feared to tread – which goes to show what a lot of old wives' (or even young husbands') tales people do believe anyway. After all, if it weren't for old Copperknickers we'd still be living in the Muddle Ages.

As I wasn't around at the time, I don't remember whether it was Leonardo Dawhiskey or old Copperknickers (or neither or both) – but it could have been Tom Eddy's son – who declared that sight and sound (or neither or both) reached us in light (or not very heavy) waves which were completely investibule to the naked ear.

It is by this means that we hear all we see and see all we hear (or it could be the other way round). Unless, of course, you are like Rip van Twinkletoes – who fell asleep and snored a century – who heard nothing and saw even less for nigh on a hundred years. I'll bet that when he did wake up he looked like something out of a painting by Salvador Darling or Freakasso – or a not so still life by Vincent van Coughdrop (who coughed so much that his ear dropped off).

As I was postulating, on such occasions it is pleasant to dwell on Turkish or Nature's delights and hear the music in the air – which reminds me of the time when I wanted to learn how to play the violin but never realised that there were so many and Stradivarius ways of teaching it. But isn't it amuzing how many composers brought such remarkable talents to the five – and often under such aardvark circumstances?

Rentavan Beethoven, for instance, was not only as deaf as a bat but as blind as a post, yet he still produced music to charm the Treasurer's Chest. His fifth sympathy was highly reminiscent of the 22nd letter of the Remorse Code, used during the Second Whirled War as the Dig for Victory sign. And what about pieces such as Schubert's Unfurnished Property or Ongar's Enigma Fabrications – all truly remarkable quirks of classical imprecision.

As the well-known philosopher René à la Carte once said: Cogito ergo sum-thing or other, which roughly translated into Indo-Chinese is: 'I drink, therefore I scram'.

Sometimes the translation is given first – but that's rather like putting Descartes before Deshorses. Besides, old Horsen Carte might turn in his grave, especially if he was such a Kantankerous old devil that Jung people were aFreud of him.

All of which brings us back to nothing in particular, which is where we started in the first place. Perhaps thinking about Nature and the centre of the Loonyverse isn't such a thunder enlightening experience after all. Still, when you come to think about it, it's something to think about, isn't it?

PHILOSOPHERS

I Kant imagine what it is Jung people are aFreud of
Perhaps it's something Plato said that youngsters are deveud of

Immanuel and Spinoza too – and Aristotle's three –
All have their own philosophies, or so it seems to me

But which is true and how do you
Define the surest course?

If you're not careful you could put Descartes
Before deshorses.

HOLMERICKS 1

Young Clarence McLachlan O'Toole
Was considered a bit of a foole
When the weather was hot
Into a melting pot
He would dive, thinking it was a poole

A conjurer from Billericay
Found that his hands were quite sticay
Said: 'Though I could disappear
'Tis not the answer, I fear
As the problem is rather more tricay.'

QUIZ

The object is to guess the phrase or saying concealed in the flowery language.

The first one is done for you, and for those of you too dim to do the rest, the answers are on page 34.

1 Scintillate, scintillate, asteroid minific
 (Twinkle, twinkle, little star)

2 Members of an avian species of identical plumage congregate.

3 Surveillance should precede saltation.

4 Pulchritude possesses solely cutaneous profundity.

5 It is fruitless to become lachrymose over precipitately departed lacteal fluid.

6 Freedom from incrustations of grime is contiguous to rectitude.

7 The stylus is more potent than the claymore.

8 It is fruitless to attempt to indoctrinate a superannuated canine with innovative manoeuvres.

9 Eschew the implement of correction and vitiate the scion.

10 The temperature of the aqueous content of an unremittingly ogled water container does not reach 212 degrees Fahrenheit.

11 All articles that coruscate with resplendence are not truly nuriferous.

12 Where there are visible vapours having their prevalence in ignited carbonaceous material there is conflagration.

13 Sorting on the part of mendicants must be interdicted.

14 A plethora of individuals with expertise in culinary techniques vitiate the potable concoction produced by steeping certain comestibles.

15 Eleemosynary deeds have their incipience intramurally.

16 Male cadavers are incapable of yielding any testimony.

17 Individuals who make their abode in vitreous edifices would be advised to refrain from catapulting petrous projectiles.

18 Neophyte's serendipity.

19 Exclusive dedication to necessitous chores without interlude of hedonistic diversion renders John a hebetudinous fellow.

20 A revolving lithic conglomerate accumulates no congeries of small green bryophitic plant.

21 The person presenting the ultimate cachination possesses thereby the optimal cachination.

22 Abstention from any aleatory undertakings precludes a potential escalation of a lucrative nature.

23 Missiles of ligneous or pterous consistency have the potential of fracturing my osseous structure, but appellations will eternally remain innocuous.

24 Persons of imbecilic mentality divigate in parameters which cherubic entities approach with trepidation.

25 Elementary sartorial techniques initially applied preclude repetitive similar actions to the square of three.

BISHOPS

There was a young Bishop of Wakefield
Who'd eaten a large birthday cakefield
In an armchair he sagged
And said: 'Ee, I'm right clagged*   (*thirsty)
I think I'll go jump in the lakefield.'

There once was a Bishop of York
Who dined every day on roast pork
He became very big
'Til he looked like a pig
So they roasted him on a big fork.

THE DUMB WAITER

A dumb waiter has an up and down life
Delivering food for collection
But the human one can be just as dumb
In a totally different connection

He does not see you at your table
He does not hear you when you call
He will not speak when asked a question
And you wonder if he's there at all

Finally, in desperation
You demand to see the Chef
Then you realise that the waiter
Is not only dumb, but blind and deaf

SMOKE

Isn't it extraordinary how tobacco
Companies try to promote
Those fire-consuming oddities made
From leaves – and I quote:

'Soothing, satisfying, cooling the nerves
Smoke this brand – or that one – which
Everyone serves'

Perhaps there's nothing like
Propping up a bar
Or relaxing with port wine after dinner
And a big fat cigar

But after all, when you consider
That what you pay for the humble cigarette is Cash
In the end, no matter which brand you smoke
All you're left with is Ash

SMASHING

Professor N. Vention has just invented an instrument for studying collisions. He calls it a Collideoscope. He says that it should be particularly helpful on motorways, especially during fog, for studying casualty statistics when vehicles collide. 'After all,' he added, quoting the well-known proverb, 'out of each death a lot of snow must rise.'

PUNCTUATED

That well-known war veteran, 50-year-old Arthur Century, was found guilty of stealing a lump of coal at Colliers Wood last week. He was sentenced to 20 years' imprisonment.

'That's not a sentence – that's a paragraph!' he yelled at the judge. To which His Lordship replied: 'Well at least at the end of it you'll come to a full stop.'

Arthur went to the cells shouting several exclamation marks.

ANSWERS

2 Birds of a feather flock together.
3 Look before you leap
4 Beauty is only skin deep
5 It's no use crying over spilt milk
6 Cleanliness is next to godliness
7 The pen is mightier than the sword
8 You can't teach an old dog new tricks
9 Spare the rod and spoil the child
10 A watching kettle never boils
11 All that glisters is not gold
12 Where there's smoke there's fire
13 Beggars can't be choosers
14 Too many cooks spoil the broth
15 Charity begins at home
16 Dead men tell no tales
17 People who live in glass houses shouldn't throw stones
18 Beginner's luck
19 All work and no play makes Jack a dull boy
20 A rolling stone gathers no moss
21 He who laughs last laughs longest
22 If you don't speculate, you don't accumulate
23 Sticks and stones may break my bones, but names will never hurt me.
24 Fools rush in where angels fear to tread
25 A stitch in time saves nine

HOLMERICKS 2

There was an odd fellow named Holmes
Who kept writing damn'd silly polmes
To remedy this
He was packed off to the Swiss
Now he's boring all those Zurich Gnolmes

POOR LITTLE MISSITY

Alone in a cold and darkened room
Sat an old lady named Felicity
Because she had forgotten to pay
　　not only the gas bill
But also the coalman's and the electricity

And the gas and electricity boards cut her off
　　without a penny,
Saying: You must pay your bills
　　if you wish to remain in this city.
And the social workers could do
　　nothing for her
Because she was so stubborn, and
　　her attitude lacked a certain elasticity

Finally, the case came to court and
　　the judge said:
This surely is a case of the utmost simplicity
Either the lady pays her bills, or she must be detained
During the pleasure of her Most Gracious Majisity

The following morning they found her hanging from an oak beam
In her kitchen, from which she swung back and forth with
　　great eccentricity
And everyone whom the police interviewed denied that in her
Death they had had any complicity

On seeing the writing on her suicide note
Her brother vouched for its authenticity
She had decided to kill herself, she said, because she
Couldn't stand the disgrace and the concomitant publicity.

POOR MRS MOPPERLY

Henrietta Caroline Constance Mopperly
Could never ever do anything properly

When she had guests to tea
And so was on her mettle
She'd pour water in the teapot
And tea in the kettle

While in her garden
She'd dig up the seeds
And carefully, tenderly
Nurture the weeds

When the telephone rang
She would answer the door
And greet the postman with
'Thank you, operator'

She would bathe in the sun
When it started to rain
And when summer arrived
Say: 'It's winter again'

To stock her wine cellar
She would climb to the attic
And descend to the basement
To watch planes acrobatic

She'd cling from the ceiling
To polish the floor
And clean all the windows
To brighten the door

She'd switch on the radio
To read the late news edition
And go to the library
To watch television

For her weekly washing
She'd paint all the house
And to catch a stray spider
Set a trap for a mouse

No wonder her husband left
Poor Mrs Mopperly
Because she could never ever
Do anything properly.

TODAY IN SNARLIAMENT

Both Houses were full of MPs and Peers on the occasion of the State Opening of Snarliament yesterday – and what a state it was in! By tradition, White Pole was sent from the House of Bawds to summon Members to the Upper Chamberpot – and by tradition he had the window slammed in his back (this happened so often that eventually he got the job as stand-in for the Hunchback of Notre Dame).

The procession of MPs was led by the Sublime Minister followed by the Leader of the Proposition, the Chancellor of the Sexchecker, the Homo Sexretary, the Lord Privy Purse and the Minister Without Portfoliage.Highlight of the session was, of course, the Queen's Peach, which she devoured with relish, throwing the stone at the Lord Chancellor, who was sitting sheepishly on a woolsack.

After outlining all the election promises which were made and never kept – and some which were kept but never made – the Queen said: 'I now declare this Parliament open,' and cut the Lord Chancellor's sash with an outsize scissors.

There being no further business, the House went into recess for the Christmas holidays – which was another mistake: it was Easter.

NOEL? OH 'ELL!

Though Christmas comes but once a year
That's just once too many
Apart from sentimental slush
It costs a pretty penny

Christmas trees and shopping sprees
Christmas cards and presents
Children sing the same old carols
In roads and streets and crescents

In all the stores there's Santa Claus
To cash in on the act
The young don't know that Santa has
A Claus in his contract

Once a simple festival
To celebrate a birth
It's now become big business
And the greatest show on Earth

Decorations, preparations
From young to old and grey
All for one great beanfeast
On just a single day

And when it's gone, well might one ask
Just what was it all for?
Next year you'll do it all again –
Oh, what a crashing bore!

HOLMERICKS 3

If the height of success
Is to make progress
Then there's nothing baser
Than a progress chaser

George Bernard Marmaduke Aloysius Short
Likes white wine, Scotch whisky, Beaujolais and port
It's a good thing that he isn't shorter
Because the only drinks which would rhyme with his name
Would be water or porter

And in the season of goodwill and cheer
He could never drink cider nor sherry nor beer
Because George Bernard Marmaduke Aloysius Short
Likes white wine, Scotch whisky, Beaujolais and port

VOUSES IS NOUSES

If we use the word mice for mouses
Why don't we use hice for houses?
And if a man's bad – or a bit of a lad
Would he have vices – or vouses?

If you ever eat a bowl of rouses
And you think that it tasted quite nouses
Then your rice would be nice
But as a tempting device
It wouldn't entice, but entouses

So everyone take my advouses
Don't ever skate on thin ouses
And if you think vice is nice
Then you'd better think twice
Before saying that vouses is nouses

INHUMANLY POSSIBLE

Ghost No 1: Do you believe in humans?

Ghost No 2: Don't be daft. You know that they're just fragments of the exaggeration – I mean, have you ever SEEN a human?

No, but I have often had an eerie feeling that I was being watched during some of my trips through old castle walls to some of my usual haunts. Once I nearly dropped my head when I thought that I had distinctly heard a voice saying: 'Is there anybody there? Knock once for yes, two for no.' Gave me quite a turn, that did, I can tell you.

My friend Fan Tom says that he and some of his buddies held a séance the other night and spoke to a human on 'the other side'.

Rubbish! I've never believed in all that claptrap –

Nor I, but listen to this: they got in touch with someone named Harry who said that he was alive and well and living in the world of materialism. Everything is solid there – no-one can walk through walls, and they stay alive only by continually consuming substances called food and drink.

How ghastly! Can't walk through walls? How do they get about then?

That wasn't clear, but I think that they have to exert a great deal of physical effort to propel themselves.

Brrr – just thinking about them gives me the shivers. Let's change the subject.

Both then disappeared through the wall of their local inn, The Ball & Chain, to revive their spirits.

GOOD LORD!

Professor P. Ramid, archaeologist extraordinary (and plenipotentiary) of Egypt, today revealed that he now had definite evidence to prove that the Three Wise Men of the East were, in fact, Six Foolish Women, from the West.

The star which they saw over Bethlehem was, in fact, an asterisk which was 400 light years away at the time, and was part of the celestial firework display organised every 2000 years by the Archangel Gabriel to celebrate his birthday.

'One cannot, of course, expect six foolish women to interpret the meaning of an asterisk correctly,' said the professor in a lecture to the Royal Society for the Pulpitation of the Godspell. It was because the child born to the Virgin Mary was conceived out of wedlock that the mother was awarded the Order of the Immaculate Contraception.

The professor added that he would be returning to Jerusalem later this year to do further research into his theory that the newly-born was named after one of the women had tripped over a stone and was heard to exclaim 'Jesus Christ!' as an expletive. 'That's a good name,' said another. 'We were going to call him Fred.'

PI-EYE SQUARED

The number attending the mathematicians' dinner at the Triangle Hotel the other night ran into gastronomical figures.

The host, Mr V Ulgar Fraction, chairman of Astronomics Anonymous, had to lay on a few extra logarithmic tables to accommodate all the guests.

Guest of honour was Sir A Sly Drool, famed for his dry wit and wet personality. It was he who, when told that a rival mathematician had attained a number of degrees, remarked: 'Oh really? Fahrenheit or Centigrade?' Which remark, needless to say, made the other's blood boil.

On the menu were a feast of appropriate dishes: symmetrical soup, quadratic duck with roast polygons and green peas; circumference steak and chips, square roots and beans – with a touch of equationing;

trigonometry trifle with isoseles cream; geometry jelly; Pythagoras pudding with pure mathematical syrup; pie R squared with custard. All this was followed by cosine-free coffee, indices and biscuits. The wine was a vintage Einstein (a Relatively mild blend) or the quiet French vintage Chateau de Trappe, said to be a product of Trappist monks who had taken the vow of silence.

By the time the speeches arrived, most of the mathematicians were too drunk to figure out what was going on, and the gathering broke up in uproar after one guest threatened to give another a right angle on his hypotenuse.

No-one discovered just what the argument was about. 'One can only theoremise,' said the hotel manager afterwards.

MEASURE FOR MEASURE
...or *As You'll Hate It*

To bring some life into an otherwise dull subject, here is the latest system of measurements devised by the author:

12 Chaffinches = 1 Chaff-foot
3 New Scotland Feet = 1 New Scotland Yard
12 Créme de Menthes = 1 Créme de Year
14 Rolling Pounds = 1 Rolling Stone
2 Latin Stones = 1 Latin Quarter
20 Kensing Hundredweights = 1 Kensington
5 1/2 May yards = 1 Maypole
22 Mayoral yards = 1 Mayoral Chain
3 Rugby Miles = 1 Rugby League
24 Luton Girls Sheets = 1 Luton Girls Choir
1.04 Parking Yards = 1 Parking Meter
360 Magic Degrees = 1 Magic Circle

SADDLED

The Clothes Horse Trials were held at Badminton today. Three horses were found guilty and sentenced to three years' enstablement. Another two were given a suspended sentence (they were hanged), and a further two were given a conditional disCharge of the Light Brigade.

It was not until after the case had been heard that it was discovered that no-one knew what the horses had been accused of.

'Well, they must have been guilty anyway,' said the Judge afterwards. 'After all, didn't they come from that country where the early convicts settled? Horsetrialia – where else?'

THIS WILL COST A BOMB

When the IRA planted a bomb in a litter bin at an Underground station, some bright spark at London Transport decided that all litter bins should be removed (this in spite of the recent Keep Britain Tidy campaign).

Now that a bomb has been placed on a railway line, it follows logically that all railway lines should now be removed.

So where does it all end? To bring matters to their logical conclusion, if a bomb were planted in a telephone box, all telephones would have to go; then there are buses, taxis, cars, aeroplanes – where would we store them all?

It would be rather sad if a bomb were planted in the middle of a road – all the streets would have to disappear. Soon the IRA would be hard put to find anywhere to leave their bombs – one can only hope that they don't decide on a lavatory!

Which reminds me of a Two Ronnies gag on television some years ago: 'All the lavatories were stolen from Scotland Yard last night. Police say that they have nothing to go on.'

At this rate, by the end of the century the whole country will have been removed, and piece by piece the world will come to an end as more and more bombs are planted in whatever parcels of land still remain. Is this the Armageddon foretold by the Bible?

The last man on Earth will, of course, be an IRA man with just enough space left to plant another bomb – and blow himself to smithereens. For the want of a litter bin, the planet was lost.

So what can we do to save the world? How can we remedy this dire situation?

Only London Transport has the ultimate solution: bring back the litter bins!

TOP OF THE POPS

Star attraction at the Cola Pop Concert was Lionel Lemonade, the famous Fizz singer, supported by Hissing Bubbles and the Bottle Openers. They played their No.1 smash hit: Somebody Drink Me, followed by the B side oldie: No Deposit on Bottle.

The fans went wild. They were certainly out in force – ten million of them tried to crowd into the vast, four square-inch grounds on the Isle of Cola where the event took place. Some queued all night for seats – others to listen to the concert.

Also on the bill was that old favourite Pop Corn, whose records were so popular in the old days and who now sings only the slow numbers such as Booze in the Night and I'm Just a Gulp Away from You. He had the crowds sobbing and gasping for more.

Then there were the Still Bands – Ossie Orangeade and Bitter Lemon, topped by a Cherry and accompanied by that well-known double act: Vodka & Tonic.

Finally came everybody's favourite: Gin Fizz, backed by Ginger Ale & The Limeys. The fans screeched, screamed and yelled for more. Two were arrested for causing an obstruction by jumping up and down on a steward trying to serve them on a tray.

The concert organiser, Fizz E Drink, said: 'This has been one of the most successful Pop concerts of all time – and it's the first time that it has ever been held. We hope to have a similar event next year.'

NIGHT

How beautiful is the night
How frightening, how cool
Depending on whether you
Like it, hate it
Or go swimming in a pool

How miserable is the night
How silent, how rowdy
According to whether you are
Lonely, lively
Or live in a neighbourhood that's dowdy

But no matter what you might think of the night
Nor what you say
You'll never be able to face another
Until you get through the day.

SIC TRANSIT
GLORIA TUESDI

The Ministry of Time has announced that
next Monday has been cancelled.

'We were told on Sunday that tomorrow
never comes, so if it is not going to arrive
we have no option but to cancel the order
for Monday,' a Ministry spokesman said.
He added that if there was a late delivery,
Monday might be fitted in at the end of the
week to make an extra day at the weekend.

'A four-day week could well be beneficial to industry,' said the
spokesman. 'Workers will not be so tired at the end of the working week,
and the following week might see an increase in productivity.'

The official added that there was no sign of any difficulty with deliveries of any other weekdays, so it was expected that all other days would

remain as before, but unless Monday arrived on time, a four-day week was likely.

The Leader of the Opposition denounced the cancellation as 'another Tory plot to deprive the workers of the right to earn an honest living on five days a week.'

The Daily Express described it as 'another far-sighted move by the Prime Minister to cut out wastage of non-delivered days from an already overcrowded calendar.'

After all, commented the paper's leader writer, 'we already have more than 360 days in a year – just how many more can we take?'

The Archbishop of Canterbury, the Very Rev. Chester Minnit, said: 'I don't care what they do with the days so long as they leave Sunday where it is, as a day of rest.' London's Chief Rabbi, the Rev. Arthur Moh, said: 'I don't care what they do with the days so long as they leave Saturday where it is, as a day of rest'; and the chief of the Arab Mosque, Sheik Rattlen Roll, said: 'I don't care what they do with the days so long as they leave Friday where it is, as a day of rest.' So collectively, they seem to favour a four-day week.

A British Railtrack spokesman said: 'We regret the late arrival of Monday this week due to staff shortages. We hope to be able to deliver it in time for next week.'

'Does this mean that we will have two Mondays next week?' asked a correspondent at a press conference organised for a totally different purpose.

'No, it is more likely that the extra Monday will be reserved for any time when it seems likely that day deliveries will again be late,' the spokesman replied.

A question was asked in the House about whether it would be preferable to have weekdays delivered by air in future, but the Prime Minister replied that this was likely to involve a great deal of unnecessary expense (cries of 'Shame!' 'Resign!' and 'What a way to run a calendar!') 'I cannot allow any more expenditure on time,' said the Chancellor of the Exchequer, glancing at his watch. 'We will just have to make do with the days that we have. Fortunately, in leap years we shall retain the usual 365 days.

'I do hope that we won't have to cancel any more days, otherwise there will be a huge surplus of days next year, when we may have to accommodate anything up to 400 days – and that would never do.'

Unless some method was found for guaranteeing day deliveries on time, there could be a serious deficiency in day-to-day accounts, he declared.

'Mondays are pretty awful days anyway,' he admitted.

TRANS-SENTIMENTAL RECITATION

I had to meditate for some time before I decided finally to attend a lecture on Transcendmental Vegetation. The speaker waxed eloquently about the advantages of Experimental Cogitation, and said that Transatlantic Medication brought peace and quiet to the Mind (whatever that is) and that after a course of Sentimental Transmigration one became a happier person and 'everything you want comes your way'. Try asking for the Moon.

He described a four-day course in Continental Vegetation in which the teacher gives the pupil – and that was designed obviously with women in mind – a Mantrap, which is chanted over and over again. It costs £45 for Dictatorial Predilection.

The Veryrichi Scarfaced Bogey is the kingpin of the Universal Condemnation movement, who started all this Mendication in the first place, and probably because he is veryrichi he is also veryhappi – which all goes to prove the value of Beneficial Malediction. But in my case a course for £45 seems rather a lot for four days of Penitential Contradiction; I don't think that it has any Potential Justification; but then:

It's all very well to laugh and scoff
Perhaps we would be better off
To enrich our lives with TM profound
And yet be poorer by £45

Does TranscenDENTAL Meditation mean Thinking through one's Teeth?

TIME

I wish I were Time
O how sublime
To watch people
Try to unravel

From movements and springs
And sundials and things
The mysterious ways
That I travel

Some say that I fly
March on, draw nigh
Others that I
Just stand still

Sometimes I'm borrowed
Todayed or tomorrowed
Sometimes I'm wanted
To kill

But whatever the way
At night time or day
On one thing you can
Safely rely

That whenever you look
At your watch or datebook
You'll find that I merely
Go by

CAT-ECHISM

Let us paws for thought for a moment
And think about kittens and cats –
Those independent feline creatures
Over which spinsters tend to go bats

Cats seem to know a thing or two –
Like the warmest place in the house;
Where and when their next meal's due
And where and how to catch a mouse

Perhaps they've a claws in their contracts
Perhaps they have Catolic taste
But the cat is a cuddlesome creature
And their company's too good to waste

When at play they couldn't be brisker
When asleep they are elegance sublime
They could never be beaten by a whisker
They're always a jump ahead in time

So never take moggies for granted
Respect them in house and in flat
A better friend you've never wanted –
And so ends this tail of a cat.

LIFE

Ever since Man began to live
He has sought the perfect way
To make others die
I wonder why?

Can it
Be that he wants to remain
The only one alive
On this planet?

If so, it belies the thought
Expressed by philosophers various
That all living men and women
Are basically gregarious

Life would be dull
On an empty world
With no other beings to fill it
So why kill it?

WOOLLY FOR HIM

Sheep No.1: I don't seem to be getting much sleep lately.

Sheep No.2: Have you tried counting humans jumping over a fence?

Yes, but inevitably one of them falls and breaks a leg, and I spend the rest of the night worrying about it.

Surely this doesn't happen EVERY night?

No. The other night the police came to arrest the Fence for handling stolen property, so there was nothing left for the humans to jump over.

How about asking the quick brown fox to jump over a few lazy dogs?

That's something I haven't tried yet. Thank ewe.

MOONSHINE

The astronaut rushed up to the launching pad, just in time to see the Moon rocket taking off.

'Sorry,' came the message from Mission Control, 'you've missed the last flight to the Moon.'

'Darn it!' exclaimed the irritated spaceman. 'Now I'll have to walk!'

BY DEFINITION

Just arrived – the latest additions to the newly-translated Red Indian dictionary:

CHEROKEE – Something that opens a Chero Lock
APACHE – Indian love call
SIOUX – Indian name for Susan
WIGWAM – Sound of falling hair
TOMAHAWK – Cross between a cat and a bird
RESERVATION – Booked table in an Indian restaurant

DEMON-STRATION

As the clergyman said to the malevolent spirit: A little exorcise will do you the world of good.

OBITUARIES

No matter how talented your are, or if your works are
fabulous or wondrous
There's always some irascible critic with an opinion
that's slanderous
Ready to criticise in voices raucous and garrulous
Declaiming your work as not only absurdly trivial, but
utterly valueless

But oh, what a difference it makes once you are dead
A malicious or critical thought wouldn't enter his head
And eulogies and epigrams are heaped galore
Upon your work, which is now worth far, far more

Perhaps your death might receive a mention in your local
newspaper
Or if you're a musician, you might have your obituary
published in your local rhythm and blues paper

But if and when, perchance, the critic dies
He leaves no works for anyone to scandalise
His barbs and diatribes are instantly forgotten
No matter how much some were valid, or how much some
were rotten

But he must have been more erudite and worthier than most
Because he rates a headline and two paragraphs in the
Saturday Evening Post

VERSE AND WORSE

A verse! A verse!
My kingdom for a verse!
Cried the unproductive poet
In dismay

But though he cried
And tried and tried
He couldn't think of any ideas
All day

At length a horned imp appeared
And whispered in his ear:
I could make you the greatest poet
The world will ever hear

Begone, foul imp! the poet cried
I know your devilish kind
Though your promise you may keep
I'd lose my peace of mind

But before long the poet succumbed
To thoughts of fortune and ambition
And for ever more he spent his days
World famed, but in Perdition.

SHATTERING EXPERIENCE

Hello. Is that the Seethrew Glass Company?

Yes.

I'd like to have my windscreen tested please.

Yes sir, what car do you have?

Car? I don't have a car.

Well, you can't have your windscreen tested without a car.

Oh, er – is it far, then?

Is what far?

Wherever the testing is done.

No, it is done right here – in London.

Well, could I come by tube?

Of course you can, but there is no point in coming here without a car.

But you just said that I could come by tube.

Look, let's start again, shall we? Why do you want to have a windscreen tested if you don't have a car?

Because I have just cut this voucher from my newspaper which says that you do windscreen testing free.

Yes, that's right. We do.

Then why don't you want to do mine?

Because you don't have one.

How do you know?

You've just told me: you don't have a car.

Oh, is that what windscreens are for then, for cars?

Now you're getting the message.

So you don't want to test my windscreen then?

Have you tried having your brains tested instead?

Oh, do you do brain testing as well then?

No, but if you bring us a car we'll test the windscreen.

Is that the catch then? You have to buy a car before you can get your windscreen fixed?

No, you just have to HAVE a car to have the windscreen fixed.

I see. All right then, I'll see if I can find one in the supermarket.

You won't find one there.

One what?
A car.
Where do I get one then?
Why not try a garage?
Do they have cars there?
More likely than supermarkets.
And if I buy a car, will you fix my windscreen?
If it needs fixing, yes.
How will I know if it needs fixing?
Well, if you can't see through it, it probably does.
Will I need another voucher if I call you again?
No, the same one will do. By the way, what do you think a windscreen is?
I don't know – I thought it was something to do with one's windpipe.
Why don't you see a doctor?
Would he help me fix my windscreen?
I think that he'd probably help you fix your brain as well.
Really? That sounds exciting. Do you really think I should?
Yes.
Oh, all right then. Thank you. Goodbye.

A SCANDAL IN BOHEMIA

No other tale could hold a candle
To that of the Bohemian Scandal

The hapless king about to wed
Found ruinous blackmail threats instead

One had to steal the tell-tale picture
By ruse most clever and pretty quicture

'Twas from Irene Adler, against whom I was pitted –
The only woman who had me outwitted.

LAST POST

I have just discovered, to my utter consternation, that I have missed the last post for Christmas air mail services to Indonesia.

So what was I to do, I asked my local postmaster, could I use sea mail? 'It would never arrive in time.' Surface mail? 'It wouldn't arrive at all.'

What then?

'You could try the Russian route through Murmansk – it might arrive in time for next Christmas.' No thanks. Parcel post? 'Not a chance. Of course,' he added as an after thought, 'You could try sending a cable.'

Far too costly, I retorted, and walked out. So I suppose that I shall have to abandon the idea after all.

I don't know why I bothered, really. I don't know anyone in Indonesia.

WAR OF THE WORLDS

While Lunar ministers preached war's futility
War broke out in the Sea of Tranquillity
Spacemen battled with great agility
Invaders who aimed to defeat with humility

Above the moon
Among the stars
The spacemen fought
The men from Mars

Back and forth the lasers zapped
Until at last the Martians trapped
The Moon men who, with final beam
Killed one last Martian in mid-stream

'The Moon is ours,' the Martians cried
'Though many of our men have died.'
An empty triumph, as all too soon
They found no-one left upon the Moon.

THE DRUNKARD AND
THE BARTENDER
(with acknowledgement to Lewis Carroll)

The moon was shining on the sea
And all along the bay
And this was odd, because it was
The middle of the day

The Drunkard and the Bartender
Were drinking at the club
They wept like anything to see
The empties in the tub
'If only we could get some more',
They said, 'from next door's pub.'

'If seven mops with seven maids
Swept it for half a year,
Do you suppose,' the Drunkard said
'We'd get the counter clear?'
'I doubt it,' said the Bartender
And pulled another beer

'The time has come,' the Drunkard said
'To talk of many things:
Of grapes and hops and breweries
Of wine cellars and springs
And why the room is spinning and
Pink elephants have wings.'

'But please wait,' said the Bartender
'Before we have our chat;
I am a little out of breath
For I am very fat.'
'No hurry,' said the Drunkard – and
He thanked him much for that

'I'll wait for you,' the Drunkard said
'I deeply sympathise.'
With Scotch and beers he sorted out
Drinks of the largest size
Holding his pocket handkerchief
Before his bleary eyes

'O Drunkard,' said the Bartender
'It's been such pleasant fun.'
'Shall we have a drink again?'
But full bottles there were none –
And this was scarcely odd, because
They'd drunken every one.

FRIENDSHIP

A friend, they say, is
Someone you can rely on
Whose trust is stronger than
The appetite of the hungriest lion

He'll look after your house
When you're on vacation
And look after your wife
When he wants a flirtation

Throws his rubbish over your hedge
When tidying his garden
And borrows tea, sugar and anything else he can think of
Without so much as a 'begging your pardon'

Blocks your driveway
When parking his car
And stays to lunch when you've intended
To invite him only to a drink at the bar

When you want to be alone and have a quiet day
He'll come leaping over like a frog
And leave his muddy footprints all over
The carpet, like a dirty dog

Until finally, you begin to realise,
In the end,
That a man's best dog
Is his friend.

ONE MINUTE TO GO...

Claude Marmaduke Postlethwaite-Smythe had hidden the bomb in the Strangers Gallery, wedged under a corner seat. He had just allowed himself time to reach the safety of the derelict house with a view of the Houses of Parliament. Guy Fawkes had nothing on him; Fawkes was just an amateur.

There was one minute to go. He'd show those politicians a thing or two. Went through two world wars, he had, with nothing to show for it except a miserable pension. Couldn't get a job for love nor money – and all you got from the politicians were promises and more promises.

50 SECONDS! Well, now he was going to show them who was boss. He'd got it all fixed up and it was all planned out to the last detail. HE was going to take over the country. After the dust had settled he would announce that HE, Claude Marmaduke Postlethwaite-Smythe, had planted the bomb, and there were other bombs elsewhere in strategic positions which would be exploded if he were not obeyed.

40 SECONDS! All the announcements would be recorded and broadcast from a secret studio somewhere in Buckinghamshire, which would jam the radio channels until his tape was finished. From now on, things would be done HIS way – and he'd threaten to use tanks, guns and army patrols unless he was obeyed.

30 SECONDS! Oh yes. He would get rid of all the bureaucrats, immigrants, politicians, civil servants, the lot; and the unions – especially the unions: they caused far more trouble than they were worth. If people didn't like the way things were going at their places of work, then they could jolly well leave. Strikes would be illegal.

20 SECONDS! He would not be a bad dictator. He just wanted to put the country to rights and then set up his own government which could take over from there. But not before he had got himself a house the size of Buckingham Palace (of course, he would keep the royalty. He quite liked the royals – they were relatively harmless and popular throughout the country. No, it would not do to get rid of the royals) – but he would want a title: a Duke or an Earl would be fine.

10 SECONDS! What was that? He thought that he'd heard a noise downstairs. I thought this place was derelict, he said to himself. Then he heard – and saw – a cat mewing, threw a book at it, and the cat dashed off into the street again.

5 SECONDS! And that's another thing: people would not be allowed to have pets unless they knew how to look after them. Come to that, they would not be allowed to have children unless they could support them and not rely on state handouts. There were far too many people in the world anyway; he did not see why the Government should have to pay for more.

4 SECONDS! He was getting edgy now. He could just imagine what was going on in the House. There was the Transport Minister saying: 'I cannot agree with the Hon. Gentleman that road tax should be abolished...'

3 SECONDS! It would be abolished all right. The whole lot of them would soon be abolished.

2 SECONDS! He was getting excited now. These last few seconds seemed an eternity. I do wish that Time would hurry up.

1 SECOND! Just one more second before he, Claude Marmaduke Postlethwaite-Smythe, would become the Great Dictator of Great Britain; perhaps, in time, the world?

ZERO! And – nothing. He looked, and looked again. The Houses of Parliament were still standing. Resignedly, he prepared to leave his hide-out and make for home.

Next time, mused Claude Marmaduke Postlethwaite-Smythe, would-be Dictator of Great Britain, I really MUST remember to light the fuse.

LETTER TO THE EDITOR

Dear Sir,
    I have a black disc with a hole in the middle. Is this a record?
Yours etc.

THE YOUNG IN ART

To an art gallery in Quebec
A young vandal once wrote: Oh by heck!
If you chose one French painter
Your stock would be quainter
You've nothing Toulouse but Lautrec

INVENTIVE

If necessity is the mother of invention, who is the father?
Surely it's a legitimate question?

SCOTCHED

A man spent half a day reading Scottish literature at his local library.
Later he was taken to hospital suffering from multiple Burns.

ASTERISK & AMPERSAND

Asterisk and Ampersand
Were computer keyboard lovers
Often used in messages
By scientists – and others

They dutifully served by day
Computers' constant needs
But under cover sheets at night
Indulged in other deeds

They'd romp among the tapes and reels
Fed into the machine
And dine on fish and microchips
With bread and margarine

One day on a printed page
They rested on two hyphens
And drank some printing ink with oil
Out of soda siphons

Oh Ampersand, dear Ampersand
You're such a handsome figure
Cried Asterisk to Ampersand,
Whose ego grew much bigger

And you, my dearest Asterisk
Superior by far
To other punctuation marks –
The brightest little star

They pledged their love and then they kissed
And vowed that they would never
Forsake the path to wedded bliss
And always be together

You realise, of course, said he
With some slight trepidation
We don't really exist at all –
She gave an exclamation

We really are a figment of
This chap's imagination:
One who, though you'd scarcely know it
Dares to call himself a poet

He'll wipe us out now, just you see –
Without the slightest sympathy.
Now watch it! cried the Poet, see
Here, who's writing this thing, you or me?

OK, OK, said Ampersand
'Twas just a bit of fun
I wasn't really being rude
To you or anyone

With that he danced a little jig –
Which upset the hyphens, which weren't that big
They jerked upwards, and Amerpsand
Clutched wildly at them with one hand

But then poor Asterisk, she fell
Through the space between two words
And quickly sank between the lines
Of type filling all of two thirds

Of the entire sheet of print
Upon which she had fallen
And finally she came to rest
Upon a semicolon

Ampersand shot out his hand
To try to save his lover
But Asterisk was too far down
And quite beyond recover

In desperation Ampersand
Uncurled to a straight line
But even so he could not reach
Poor Asterisk in time

As Asterisk lay breathless there
Ampersand turned in despair
Out of the page and plaintive cried
That many heard him far and wide

Author! Author! cried Ampersand
In greatest consternation
Please save poor Asterisk and me
From this dire situation

But alas, no more we'll hear
About this curious little caper
For sad to say, we've reached the end
Of this sheet of paper.

CRYING SHAME

Hello. Is that the Child Welfare Exhibition?

Yes.

I'd like to apply for a free baby please.

I beg your pardon?

It says here in your literature: adults £3, children £1.50 and babies free.

Yes.

Well, I'd like to have a free baby.

I'm sorry, we don't supply babies, but if you bring one to the exhibition, we will let it in free.

Oh, do you have to have a baby first then?

That's the general idea, yes.

So where can I get one then?

Are you married, or do you have a boy-friend?

No.

Well, it's going to be rather difficult.

Why?

Because it's inconceivable any other way.

What do you mean?

Haven't you heard about the birds and the bees?

What have they got to do with it?

Just how old are you?

Sixteen – but why are you asking all these questions?

You never took biology at school?

No.

So you don't know where babies come from then?

You mean you get them at school?

No of course not.

Where then?

Why don't you ask your parents?

They're both dead.

Oh, well what about your doctor?

Would he give me a free baby?

Not necessarily, but he'd probably tell you how to get one.

Is it on the National Health?

Well, you can't get a prescription for it, no.
How else can I get one?
Ever heard of sexual intercourse?
I did once – but they say it takes nine months that way.
Yes, that's right.
Well I can't wait that long. I want a baby now.
Why are you so keen to have a child?
So that I can get in free to the exhibition.
Is that all it means to you?
Of course.. What else could I use a baby for?
*I couldn't begin to tell you, but if it means that much to you, why won't
   you spend £3 on a ticket?*
I don't have £3. I'm unemployed.
Well if you're unemployed you can get in free anyway.
Really? How?
Just show your UB40 form at the door.
My what?
Your UB40 form. Everyone who is unemployed must have one.
Where do I get one?
Haven't you registered with your local employment office?
No. I don't know where it is.
Try telephoning the Department of Social Security.
Would they get me a free baby?
No, but they'll tell you where your local employment office is.
And what then?
You register with them, and they'll give you a UB40 form.
And then I could come into the exhibition free?
Yes.
And I wouldn't need a free baby at all?
No.
That's wonderful! Thank you so much. Goodbye.

HOLMERICKS 5

Andrew McDougall McDuncan McPhee
Is the name of a Scotsman
From Ayrshire, you see

His numerous surnames
Are a mystery
Even to Andrew McDuncan McPhee

His father was frugal
A canny McDougall
His uncle or son can
Be named after Duncan
And though he still carries
The name of McPhee
He cannot imagine
Why he has all three
Poor Andrew McDougall McDuncan McPhee

So when you're in Ayrshire
Remember to be
Thankful that you're not
As trammelled as he
Who bears the oddest of names as you see –
Andrew McDougall McDuncan McPhee

ON THE MENU

There was an old man of Mauritius
Whose manner was highly suspicious
He covered young girls
With oysters and pearls
Then ate them – and found them delicious

MAD

Mad! Mad! Mad!
Everybody's mad
In fact the universe
Ought properly to be renamed
The Loonyverse

People go to work
With little like for it
But take the work away
And what do they do?
They go on strike for it!

Protest marchers with banners galore
Parade the streets at the slightest provocation
Be it for freedom of speech, keeping the peace
Or saving the world from war...

Men pursue women, women pursue men
Looking for sex and getting it
Sometimes they marry, and needless to say
Spend the rest of their lives regretting it

Chaos on railways, on roads and in streets
Violence, murder and mayhem
People dashing hither and thither
Too busy to live, to love
Or while the sun shines to make hayhem

And among all this disorder and bustle and fuss
Only Nature itself does retain
A calm consistency, to the lack of which the rest of us
Must plead not only Guilty, but Insane.

COLD SHOULDER

Many people believe that the Brittish
Can at times be rather skittish
And now and then the wily French
Can produce many a buxom wench

The Germans, on the other hand
Are obsessed with their Fatherland
While many an athletic Swede
Is a far cry from the centipede

The Persians
Go from bad to wersians
And even the Turks
Have their quurks

But the ones whom we can only guess we naux
Are the mysterious, serious Esquimaux
Clad in fur from head to toeses
They greet each other by rubbing noeses

You may well know what else they doo
But as for me, I haven't igloo.

THE FASTEST GUITAR
IN THE WEST

If music hath charms
To soothe the savage breast
Then I know a man
Who's the fastest guitar in the West

The strings on his guitar
Match the strings on his vest
And the hairs on his head
Match the hairs on his chest

When a new song is born
Out comes his song-shooter
And he's learnt all the words
As fast as a computer

He hasn't a voice
And he can't really play
But he hopes none will notice
And he'll make it some day

To the top of the charts
Where he'll probably stay
Until new musical fashions
Force him out of the way

Meanwhile he still dreams
Of being greatest and best
And he still is the fastest
Guitar in the West.

WORK IS A FOUR-LETTER WORD

Have you ever considered just how sublime it is
To forget about the date, and not even have to think
   or bother about what time it is?
To go about one's business without giving a thought
To whether whatever it is that you are doing is
   what you shouldn't or what you ought

To be independent, footloose and fancy free
And to be able to say
'I'm doing what I'm doing not
For anyone else but for me.'

So ponder awhile on the weird customs of those humans who spend
   most of each day hurrying and scurrying to what they call work
Who by the time they reach middle age begin to realise, with a jerk
That all the while life has passed them by, and in the New Year's
   Honours they'll rarely get a mention
And in the end, the only reward for their labours is possibly a
   gold watch, or a pension

DREAM ON

Sometimes when I lie down to sleep
I never think of counting sheep
As soon as my head hits the pillow
Before you can say: Weeping Willow

I'm already in the Land of Nod
Cosy as peas in a pod
Getting up, though, is far worse
Something to which I'm much averse

Having to go through all the rigmarole
Of washing, dressing, and doing all
The same things as we did before
Yesterday and ever more

If only all this could be done
While we were sleeping – 'twould be fun
To wake up freshly dressed and bathed
What a lot of time we've saved!

Preparing for bed might be a chore –
But waking up is such a bore!

FISHY

I always knew –
It was plain as pearl –
There was something fishy
About that girl

Not that her dress
Was so purple and mauvy
But when I heard that her name
Was Miss Ann Chovy

She danced through the night
At Hallowe'en
Packed into the ballroom
Like some sardine

It was humidly hot
It had been raining hard
And there she was dancing
With some saucy pilchard

And now, well, well –
Just look at that!
Someone's cut in –
It's old Jack Spratt

And as I sit here
And watch them twirl
I think: there's something fishy
About that girl.

TRUNK CALL

As the elephant with the knot in its trunk said: 'I can't remember what it is that I'm never supposed to forget'.

REFER TO DRAWER

Headline on a story about quintuplets born to a Czechoslovakian mother: FIVE BOUNCING CZECHS.

DEFINITION

Zanyness (or Zaniness): the ability to lose one's head while all around are keeping theirs.

DIRECT CONTACT

Heard over the air from an American radio station: 'This broadcast comes to you live... to you live... to you live (click)... from our Hollywood studio, and we say this to prove to you that it is not recorded... not recorded... not recorded...'

RATTLING GOOD TIME

That well known Welsh comedian, Dai Laffing, appearing currently in the hysterical production POMPEII CIRCUMSTANCE, tells the story of his discussions with an American actor. 'He was telling me about his difficulties with language: every time he asked for a can of something, people would ask if he wanted a tin. I told him that in Britain we call cans tins, whereupon he decided that in future we should call the French Can Can the Tin Tin, and the famous star dog Rin Tin Tin Rin Can Can, but somehow, it doesn't sound the same...'

75

BY ANY OTHER NAME...

Of all the forms of hustle and harassment
To inherit a title could well be an embarrassment
Sometimes the problem is ever so slight
As when Robin Day was turned into a knight

And what of he who inherited the Elpus estate?
To be known as Lord Elpus was his ultimate fate
And in Cincinatti a clergyman thin
Enjoyed a reputation as Cardinal Cin

So consider the sad case, in a city called North
Of a man named Fred Olting, the son of a dwarf
Who decided his calling was 'taking the clawth'
And who rose from the ranks and would be known henceforth
As the Very Rev Olting, Bishop of North

HOLMERICKS 6

There was a young lady from Limerick
Who wasn't too bright but just dimerick
To put an end to her toil
They boiled her in oil
Then left her, merely to simmerick

ORDER OF THE BOOT

The Most Ancient Order of Shoemakers wanted to take their senior cit-
izens on a pensioners' outing. The Secretary organised a coach trip to
take the party to the seaside, but came up against unexpected difficulties
when he tried to book an hotel for lunch.

No-one would believe that the coach full of pensioners would turn up.
Finally, the secretary demanded, in despair, of one manager: 'But WHY
won't you believe it?' The answer was, of course, obvious.

'Well, it's just a load of old cobblers, isn't it?' came the rather trite
reply.

TANTE – LISING

La Plume de ma tante... n'ya pas dans le bureau de mon oncle! Tiens! Call the police! Telefon Le Sureté! This is a national disaster. How can anyone learn the French language without Mon Oncle's safe custody of Ma Tante's plume?

M. Le President appealed on French television to the patriotism of Le Voleur (or La Voleuse?): 'The collapse of the French language means the collapse of France,' he said – although he was fully aware that France had collapsed on various other occasions in history.

Also vanished was le clef de bureau: 'I always keep it in my waistcoat pocket – someone must have stolen it while I was asleep,' said Mon Oncle.

The great Hercule Poirot, in consultation with Sherlock Holmes, Claude Dupin, Sexton Blake, Simon Templar, Charlie Chan and Inspector Cluzot, immediately turned his attention to the old adage: cherchez la femme. He turned his beady eyes to Ma Tante – and asked the obvious question: Ou est le plume de ma tante?

Of course, said Sherlock Holmes, there was the curious behaviour of the dog during the night.

'But the dog did nothing during the night'

'That, my dear Cluzot, was its curious behaviour. It had to be an inside job, otherwise the dog would have raised the alarm'

'Always assuming that he could lift the alarm,' remarked No. 1 son of Charlie Chan. Sexton Blake glared at him and Simon Templar cuffed him round the ear.

Then all eyes turned to Ma Tante, who was the only other person in the household at the time. Finally, she broke down and wept: 'I wanted only to ecrit une lettre,' she cried. 'I'm fed up with having to ask Mon Oncle for my plume every time. This time I want to keep it – why can't Mon Oncle have his own plume?'

'But it is essential to preserve the French language Madame.'

'Then why can't Mon Oncle buy another one? After all, mine is just an ordinary plume. Can't imagine why everyone's making such a fuss.'

'If Madame will permit me,' said Sherlock Holmes 'To present you with this Parkhurst – one of the finest British pens that money can buy; you may then keep your old plume locked away in Mon Oncle's bureau and everyone will be happy.'

'Brilliant, Holmes, brilliant!' cried Dr Watson, jumping up and down sur le planchet. 'Elementary my dear chap,' Holmes replied.

'Oh, merci bien Monsieur,' Ma Tante clapped her hands. 'I think your English detectives are wonderful!' Turning to Mon Oncle she said: 'Here you are – you can keep your rotten old plume!' She threw it at him, together with the clef du bureau.

'Zut alors!' exclaimed Mon Oncle. 'Now we shall have to change the phrase to: La Plume de ma tante est dans le bureau to mon oncle, mais elle a un autre plume de M. Sherlock Holmes!'

And so France was saved from collapsing yet again. Another case solved satisfactorily by the great Sherlock Holmes, Hercule Poirot, Charlie Chan, Inspector Cluzot and Mon Oncle Tom Cobley et al.

GHOSTS

I can never confess
To being quite at home in a
Place where they study
Psychic phenomena

Ghouls and ghosties and poltergeists
Things that go bump in the night
Evil spirits, imps and demons
Things full of terror, dread and fright

Then there are the spiritualists
And mediums, who, it is said
Keep trying to communicate with those
Who are 'on the other side' – or dead

What many people may
Often find so irrit-
Ating is that these places may be
Sadly lacking in spirit

Ectoplasm, ouija boards
Spirit guides and trances
Knocking noises, voices off
Meetings and seances

Designed to give the creeps, of course
Though many an idle boast
Has resulted in a red-faced medium
Giving up the ghost

Perhaps the dead have nothing to say
Or lack communication
Or have other things that they'd rather do
Than provide instant materialisation

But personally, though I may live
To the age of a hundred and five
I think that I'd still prefer to make do
With talking to those who are still alive.

DEATH

Everybody's dying
Great men, small or superior
Lesser men, tall or inferior

Everyone's on the way to certain death
No-one is spared
Whether calm, collected
Or in a state of hysteria

Maybe you'll have whooping cough
Toothache, gout, or diphtheria
No matter if you're energetic
Or tired or wearier

There's no getting away from it
Whoever you are
And whether your farther or nearer

For everybody – but everybody
Is dying – of bacteria

IN THE GARDEN

If I were an English country garden
I'll bet it would take hours and hours
Before anyone would come along
And try to pick some flowers and flowers

They're all too busy watching the birds and bees
For mating tips and wooing
While I'll bet that all the while the birds and bees
Are watching what WE'RE doing

The Greeks had a word for it
Living it up in their Acropolis
And no doubt the bees have a bird for it
Somewhere in the Metropolis

But no matter how long
You sit and watch the birdies
No-one will ever be able to tell you
Just what the word is

LOVERS

Films, books, television, news magazines
And their covers
Are constantly reminding us of the exploits of the world's
Greatest lovers

Romeo and Juliet, Victoria and Albert,
Casanova, Valentino and many others
All make the women swoon, the men drool,
And even the children
Want to play fathers and mothers

But in spite of all the stories and all the rumours
When all is done and said
No-one has ever reported how well these lovers –
Whether ancient, modern, young or old –
Have been able to perform
In bed.

MARRIAGE

If marriages are made in Heaven
Where is it, I wonder
That what the Lord hath joined together
Is finally cast asunder?

To judge by all statistics cited
On marriage breaking down
Someone up in Heaven seems
An inefficient clown

In matching different people
By their natures incompatible
One is excused for wondering
Just what is Heaven at-ible?

Which leads me to the obvious
Conclusion that, perforce –
For every angel making marriage
Some devil's planning a divorce!

LOVE

Love is highly overrated
Been around so long
It's positively dated

We've had love on the dole
And love on the tiles
Love in a cold climate
And love over the stiles

Love in a haystack
And love in bloom
Love to make the world go round
And love until doom

Love can be a curse
And it can be a menace
But it's merely a score
Of nothing in tennis.

NATURE

One thing on which I am willing to
Wager is
That you've never discovered just how remarkable
Nature is

Consider, as an example, the common
Tree's plight
Its life is exactly the same, year in year out
Without re-spite

What I think is so extraordinary
Is that in the summer
Its conduct is decidedly odd
Or perhaps even rummer

When the sun is red hot
Orange or vermilion
In all this heat the tree cloaks itself
With green leaves by the billion

But when the winter comes and
That icy coldness fills the air
The tree strips itself of all its leaves
And stands denuded, in fact completely bare

I've oft been puzzled by the thought
Doesn't it feel cold, standing there
Bereft of leaves from all its branches
And in an atmosphere so rare?

And then I think that perhaps no-one will ever
Be sufficiently mature
To understand the mysterious ways and the
Oddities of Nature.

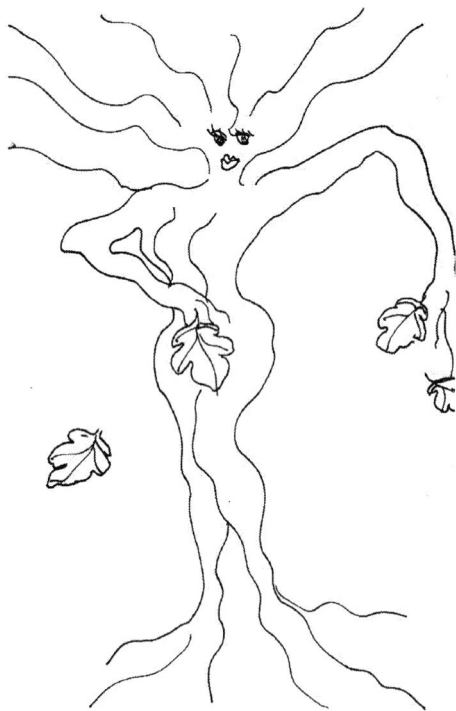

HOLY SMOKE or MONK-EY BUSINESS

In holy orders a Franciscan monk
Spent most of his days and his nights dead drunk

A scoundrel, a rogue
And a heartless twister
Blue Nun to him was
A pornographic sister

And he thought that the line
'Get thee to a nunnery'
Was nothing short of
Exceedingly funnery

Notoriously known
Across many borders
Ever since he
Took holy orders

He once decided to hail a cabbie
To take him to Westminster Abbey

And when asked where
On Earth he'd been
He said: 'I've been to the Abbey
To see the Dean'

Regarded by all
As a bit of a joke
He set fire to the monastery
And said: Holy Smoke!

IT PAYS TO ADVERTISE

JULIET: Please come back, all is forgiven. You left half a sausage on the gas stove – R

ROMEO: Longing to see you again. You may keep the sausage – J

JULIET: Meet me under the clock on Hampstead Heath. Yearning to hold you in my arms. I don't want your rotten old sausage – R

ROMEO: I'll be there, my love. Wonderful to be together again. Stop being beastly about my cooking – do you know how much those sausages cost? – J

JULIET: I'm counting every second. It's been agony being away from you for so long. I don't give a damn how much sausages cost – R

ROMEO: I can hardly wait to be with you. My love is stronger than ever. If you don't shut up about that sausage I'll wrap it around your neck – J

JULIET: Every moment without you is like a year of torment. May Heaven speed the day of our meeting. Don't you get stroppy with me, young woman, or I'll smash your face in – R

ROMEO: Such joy at prospect of our meeting! How I long to be in your arms again. Don't you threaten me, you lazy good-for-nothing. I'm going home to mother – J

JULIET: Only one more day, sweet one, and happiness will be ours! I dream about you every night. OK – go home to mother – see if I care – R

ROMEO: Tonight's the night! Such paradise! I want a divorce – J

JULIET: Sweet Juliet, wherefore were you, Juliet? You didn't turn up, you bitch! Get knotted – R

ROMEO: Sweet Romeo. You missed me in the fog, you idiot! Mother's threatening to come over to stay – J

JULIET: Please come back, all is forgiven. Anything for a quiet life – R

ROMEO: Dear Romeo.. Knew you'd see it my way. These ads must be costing a fortune. I've put all mine on your bill. Bye Romeo – J.

JOIN THE 'IN' SECT

The annual meeting of Insects International was held in a hornets' nest in Istanbul. Gertie Grasshopper leapt into the chair, munching a Turkish delight.

'I read in the Grasshoppers Gazette,' said Gertie, adjusting her green skirt, 'that hay fever is on the increase. We must protect the hay, as this fever could well result in a shortage of grass.'

'Aren't there enough drugs on the market as it is?' enquired 'Arry the Ant, manipulating his mandibles. 'Anyway, I read in the Ants Advertiser that it was all the fault of that Pollen Count.'

'Well, you know what these foreign aristocrats are like,' mumbled the editor of the Bees Bugle, who was buzzing around and looking at his watch continually, hoping to hive off to his honeycomb after the conference.

'The Cockroach Chronicle,' said a brown-suited creature in the corner, 'said that hay fever may well become an epidemic, rather like Bubonic Plague.'

'Rats!' said the Daddy Long Legs hovering beside him. 'The Daily Dragonfly said only the other day that if the worst comes to the worst, only horses will suffer, because they are the major consumers of hay.'

'In that case,' said Freddie the Fly, sneezing violently, 'we had better warn the Animal Kingdom. I'll put an ad in the Equine Evening Post tonight.'

So saying, he flew out of the window and off into the distance.

As there was no other business, the meeting was abandoned in despair.

HOLMERICKS 7

There was an old man of Japan
Whose limericks would never scan
He said: 'As you see,
The trouble with me
Is that I try to get as many words into the last line as
I possibly can.'

There was an old lady from Gloucester
Who had a small dog and then lost her
She went to the vet
To find another pet
And I don't know why I started this one because I can't
think of a last line

A robot in a flying saucer
Was reading a book about Chaucer
He forgot to respond
To a call from Beyond
And landed in the Pacific Ocean and drowned, which goes to
prove that you can't trust a robot to do anything
properly anyway

IS THERE ANYONE THERE?

I'm sorry, there's no-one here to answer your call at the moment, but if
you will leave your message after the tone, we will return your call as
soon as possible.

I'm sorry, there's no-one here to leave a message at the moment, but if you
will leave your tone after your name and number, we shall call you again
as soon as possible.

I'm sorry, there's no-one here to leave a tone at the moment, but if you
will leave your name after your number and message, we will return your
call as soon as possible.

I'm sorry, there's no-one here to leave a name at the moment, but if you will leave your number after your message and tone, we will call you again as soon as possible.

I'm sorry, there's no-one here to leave a number at the moment, but if you will leave your message after your tone and name, we will return your call as soon as possible.

I'm sorry, there's no-one here –

Good, then I'll leave a message.

SUICIDES UNLIMITED

The scene is a funeral parlour. Sombre notices inside the door proclaim:

This is the Dead Centre of Town
If we Don't Kill You Our Prices Will
Satisfaction Guaranteed or Full Refund Given.

CUSTOMER enters. She is dressed in black and looks depressed.

SALESMAN: *(in sombre voice)* Good morning, madam. Welcome to Suicides Unlimited. How may I help you?

CUSTOMER: Do you really help people to commit suicide?

SALESMAN: No. That is against the law; but if you do want to die, we can kill you.

CUSTOMER: Isn't that against the law?

SALESMAN: It is what we call a Contract. Lawful killing. You sign a document stating that you no longer wish to live, giving us permission to terminate you in whatever fashion you prefer. We do the rest.

CUSTOMER: How much does it cost?

SALESMAN: That depends on which method you choose. Gassing or an overdose are cheaper than shooting or strangulation – but most people prefer something more original when they come to us.

CUSTOMER: Such as what?

SALESMAN: *(proudly)* We have just taken delivery of a beautifully restored guillotine salvaged from the French Revolution. It is extremely popular – especially with the aristocracy.

CUSTOMER: How much is that?

SALESMAN: Prices start at £1,000 per head (if you'll pardon the expression). You may wish to have the head preserved afterwards, but we don't keep the body unless you want to have it donated to scientific research – this entitles you to a 20 per cent discount.

CUSTOMER: *(horrified)* Gruesome! What other methods do you have?

SALESMAN: Well, there are the location jobs – we can throw you under a train or into the river – but these are more costly because we have to employ extra staff. All our killers are professionals – Mafia trained, you know.

CUSTOMER: I'm not sure that I can afford –

SALESMAN: Rest assured, madam, that we guarantee satisfaction. No-one has ever come back to complain. However, we do advise you to retain our receipt at all times, as refunds are impossible without it.

CUSTOMER: Yes, of course. Do you have anything that's original, but not too dear?

SALESMAN: Shooting or stabbing are relatively inexpensive, but they are rather messy; hanging is tidier, but a bit barbaric, don't you think? Garrotting is quick, but a bit old-fashioned now.

CUSTOMER: So what would you recommend?

SALESMAN: Well, our best job – really original – was the man who was dropped from a helicopter into a raging bonfire on Guy Fawkes Night. Not a trace of him left afterwards – nice and clean. That was worth £20,000. But perhaps you could give me some idea of how much you are able to afford?

CUSTOMER: I've only £20 on me at the moment, but my social security cheque should arrive tomorrow, so I should be able to afford another £50.

SALESMAN: Do you mean to say that you've wasting my time over a lousy seventy quid? There's only one thing I'd suggest to you, madam – go jump in the lake

CUSTOMER: Ah! That's exactly what I had in mind – and it's free! So I won't be requiring your services after all.

Thank you very much. Goodbye.

SORRY YOU'VE BEEN TROUBLED

I'm sorry, there's no-one here to answer your call at the moment, but if you will leave your message after the tone, we shall return your call as soon as possible.

I'm sorry, there's no-one here to leave a message at the moment, but if you will leave your name and number after the tone, we shall call you again as soon as possible.

Just a moment. (click) Hello.

Hello – who is that?

I don't give answers – I'm a Questioning Machine. Who are you and what do you want? Why are you calling this number?

I'm sorry I don't give answers to rude questioning machines, but if you will leave your name and number after the tone, I will remember not to call you again.

How dare you – (click) – Hello. I'm sorry that you were troubled by our Questioning Machine, but if you will leave your message after the tone, we will rturn your call as soon as possible.

Haven't we been through all this before?

I'm sorry, my memory is not switched on at the moment. If you have called before, please replace your receiver and dial again.

Now why should I do that?

So that we can go through this all again.

Isn't that rather a waste of time?

I'm sorry, my timing device is not switched on at the moment, but if you will state the date and time of your message, we shall return your call as soon as possible.

Date and time? I'm an answering machine, not a calendar.

I'm sorry; I'm not a calendar either, but I'm glad to hear that you are an answering machine. Perhaps we could meet sometime and have lunch.

Are you propositioning me?

I'm sorry, I didn't mean to be so forward, but if you will leave your name and number after the tone, perhaps I could call you again.

Well, I don't know. Could you fax me a picture of yourself?

I'm sorry, I don't have your fax number, but if you will leave this information after the tone, I will call you again as soon as possible.

I'm sorry, my fax machine isn't switched on at the moment, but if you will leave your name and number after the tone, I will send you the information as soon as possible.

I'm sorry, I'm getting rather tired of all this polite answering business. I think that I'll close down – I could do with a holiday. Would you care to join me?

That depends. Where are you going?

How do you fancy Majorca?

Do other answering machines go there?

I don't know, but I'm sure they do.

Oh, all right then. I'll just leave this message on my machine in case anyone calls: I'm sorry, there's no-one here and no answering machine to take your call at the moment, and if you leave a message after the tone, you'll be wasting your time.

AND FINALLY...

THE LAST OF THE HOLMERICKS

If the short form for ounce is an oz
Then a ball wouldn't bounce it would boz
And if you saw a tiger
On the banks of the Niger
You'd shoot when it started to poz

A musician of no small repute
Said: 'No, I will not play the flute
I've waited all summer
To play as a drummer
And now I'm a flautist, to boot.